All My Strength

My Journey From 333 To The Chicago Marathon

Eddie Robbins

DEDICATION

To my wife, Cathy and my 3 daughters, Marie, Missi
and Tiffany.

CONTENTS

333 pounds to the Chicago Marathon. From buttons busting on a shirt to crossing my legs like a girl. I have no products to sell...just a story to tell. For some of you, it has been a lifelong battle with no hope in sight. Trust me, I have been there and there *is* hope. If I can do it, you can too. I am reminded of a scene in my favorite movie, *The Apostle*. The Apostle EF, played by Robert Duval, came upon an Episcopal priest christening a boat. He said "you do it your way and I do it mine, but together, we get it done." You may not lose the weight by using my method, but hopefully you will be motivated to lose the weight your way and together we'll get it done.

If the Bible contained only one verse, John 3:16, it would be enough information for us to secure an eternal life with Jesus Christ. However, we also need to understand the context of this verse and other teachings and commandments that Christ has for us in order to live a fruitful life. So, it is with my story. Exercise 30 minutes a day and lower your calorie and fat intake. That's all you need to do, but like the Bible, there is much more to it. I do not pretend to be an expert, but will share with you what happened to me. ***If my story motivates you to attempt anything that I discuss, you MUST consult with a doctor before you begin a program..***

My story is not one of a diet plan, but one of a transformation through a renewed mind. It is a story of living a life of total disgust, experiencing a crisis moment and making a life changing decision. It is a story of how I came to understand the passion of loving the Lord with *All My Strength!*

Mark 12:30-31

Romans 12:2

2 A LITTLE BIT ABOUT ME

I grew up in Roswell, Georgia. I am the son of Loyd and Elsie Robbins. My Dad was a pastor in the Church of God (Cleveland, Tennessee). I have 2 sisters, Betty and Patricia. I went to Roswell High School and later attended Lee College where I met my wife, Cathy.

Cathy and I were married in December of 1975 at the North Cleveland Church of God. It was a wonderful, small family wedding. At least as small as it could be considering Cathy is one of twelve children. Life moved on from there. We moved to Atlanta in 1976 and back to Cleveland in 1977 and back to the Atlanta area in 1980. Cathy and I have 3 wonderful, beautiful daughters. Edna Marie was born on November 10, 1977. Melissa Michelle (Missi) was born on October 21, 1979. Tiffany Diane was born on October 5, 1983.

I weighed 235 when we married and quickly gained weight after that. It seems as though most people gain weight after they marry. I was certainly no different. I don't really remember all the details of how my weight got to 300, but it did in a few short years.

Through the years, I have probably lost thousands of pounds. I attempted several different types of diets. The most I ever weighed was 333 pounds in 1999. For most of my adult life, I have averaged 290-300 pounds. I lived a very frustrating life of losing and gaining weight. The most success I ever had with a diet was in 2000 when I lost 80 pounds on the Atkins Diet. The Atkins Diet was a very popular low-carb diet that helps you lose while still enjoying foods such as meats, eggs and cheese.

Of course, I gained most of the weight back. That is the challenge with diets. How many times have you known someone who lost weight and gained it all back? Most every time. The odds are stacked against us. That is a great motivation for me to keep the weight off. I realize that most people think I will gain the weight back but I will prove them wrong. I will keep it off. As you read my story, you will see that I am a changed man.

3 THE DAY THAT CHANGED MY LIFE

One of the questions asked of me frequently concerning my dramatic weight loss is "what made you decide to do that?" After living 30 years of averaging a weight of about 300 pounds, it is understandable that people are curious. What makes a person change? I can only tell what happened to me. It happened on July 16, 2009. I call that the day that changed my life. Of course, several events led up to this day.

In March 2009, we went on our annual family cruise. If you have ever been on a cruise you know that there is no shortage of good food. I always gain weight on a cruise. It is expected. When we got home from the cruise, my weight was 302. It was time to go on another diet. I did my routine low-carb diet and began to drop weight just like I always did. The first few pounds are always the fastest to come off. This was no exception. Over the Spring, I lost 15 pounds. That was par for the course. I wasn't excited about it but was losing back to the upper

280s which was lower than my average weight over the last 30 years. Not too bad.

On July 14, 2009, I had my annual physical. I have been very faithful getting annual physicals. I am a believer in it. On this day, I was feeling pretty good because my weight was down a bit. My regular doctor had taken a different position and was no longer at the office so I had a new doctor. Dr. Brown did my physical that day. After the exam, he questioned me about my life and my weight goals. I told him my story of being overweight all my life and how I would like to lose weight. I was saying what I think he wanted to hear. He asked me "what weight goal would you like to reach?" I told him 250 sounded good. I had to say something and randomly picked 250. He told me that was a great goal and that I could live a long, healthy life at that weight if I took care of myself. That made me feel good except for one thing. I hadn't been 250 in over 30 years. It was almost an unrealistic dream but I went along and we continued to talk. At this point, he made "the" statement. It was one of those statements that clicked with me and I give it the credit for being the beginning of my wakeup call. Dr. Brown said "you know......the first symptom of a heart attack is a heart attack." I heard bells and whistles go off in my head. I don't remember anything he said after that. It was one of those "wow" moments. It may not be that way for you, but for me, it nailed me. That statement stuck with me and still does to this day.

I think another reason Dr. Brown's statement hit home with me was the realization that I am not young anymore. My Dad passed away at age 53 and I was 54. This is the real deal. My wife and children never knew my Dad. They would have loved him. He would have loved them. He didn't take care of himself. Is this what I want for me? I want to be alive to enjoy my grandchildren. This is serious. I had to do something.

I was introduced to the great motivational speaker, Jim Rohn, through Success Magazine. In each Success Magazine, there is a CD with various speakers. My favorite was Jim Rohn. If you are not familiar with Jim Rohn's work, do yourself a favor and research him. His website is www.jimrohn.com. What a wonderful man he was. On July 16, I began to listen to one of the clips on the Success Magazine CD. It was Jim Rohn talking about living the day that changes your life. Can I change my life? I had to change my life.

Mr. Rohn talked about the greatest day of your life is the day you have "had it." It is the day you realize that you are totally disgusted with your life. Along with the statement Dr. Brown made, still resonating with me and realizing I am older than my Dad when he died, Jim Rohn had just messed with my emotions. This was it. I lost it. I began to cry and yell at myself for being fat. I hit rock bottom and spent the whole day reflecting on the disgust I had with myself.

I was mad at me. How did I allow myself to get this way? I began to go through all of the excuses. None of them were valid. Then I screamed "I am done." I hit a level of disgust that caused me to make a decision. "I am never going to be fat again," I screamed. I am done with losing 30 pounds and gaining 35. I am tired of it. I am sick of it.

By the end of July 16, 2009, I was a changed man. I hadn't lost one pound yet but I was never going to be fat again. I had decided. I felt a burden lift. It was almost a spiritual experience. Maybe it was a spiritual experience. I discovered Mark 12:30-31. I am going to love God with all my heart, soul, mind and strength. *All My Strength.*

I lived the day that changed my life. It was July 16, 2009. I will never forget that day. Can one day of an emotional experience really be the catalyst for a changed life? I have lost weight before. I am an expert at it. What is different about this experience? Time will tell.

4 I HAVE DECIDED...NOW WHAT?

I have decided to lose weight and never be fat again. Great....now what? After making the decision to lose weight, I needed a plan. I had always heard that walking was a great exercise and my daughters were always telling me I should walk so I started walking at the North Georgia Outlet Mall, six miles from our house in Dawsonville, Georgia. I walked every sidewalk one way and then back for a total of 45 minutes. Time went by very fast because of the storefronts and people to watch. I realized I needed more of a specific plan for walking so I decided to walk 25 miles a week. Why 25 miles? I don't know. It sounded serious so I went for it.

There are a couple of places that I walked. One was Rock Creek Park in Dawsonville. The track is 1.1 miles around. The other place was Central Park in nearby Cumming. That track is about a mile around. When it was too cold, I went into the gym at Central Park. There is a track around the gym that takes 12 laps to complete a mile. That can be boring but it sure beats the treadmill and the extreme cold. I began the journey of walking 25 miles a week.

Some essentials to the success of my walking was music and good shoes. I have plenty of songs on my iPhone that helped me enjoy walking. Sometimes it was inspirational walking with Chris Tomlin, David Crowder Band, Phil Keaggy, the North Point Band and Leigh Nash. Other times it was "roll back the clock" with Chicago and Toto. Did I mention that I love Chicago? Being a trumpet player, Chicago has always been my favorite band.

Good running shoes are very important. Cathy bought a pair of Saucony Guide II shoes that I enjoyed. Real running shoes made me feel that I was official. I loved my Saucony shoes. That doesn't mean they would be good for everybody. Each person has to find their favorite shoes. If you are a beginner, don't miss the importance of good shoes. In fact, it is recommended to get fitted with shoes at a running store. I did that later.

At the same time I was walking, I began a low-carb diet since it is the diet in which I was the most familiar. It was easy for me to maintain a low-carb diet. After walking for several weeks, I found myself not eating very much. Walking changed my metabolism. I decided that if I am not eating much, low-carb didn't make sense because energy comes from carbs. So, I made the change to low fat and low calories. I was a novice at healthy eating. This meant that I could add fruit and veggies back into my eating habits. I never counted fruit against my calorie intake. It also meant that I could do smoothies for recovery after long walks. I was satisfied with this plan. In fact, I enjoyed it. I still do.

For fun, when I arrived at my walking destination, I always scouted out the other people who were walking. My goal was to out-walk them. If they were on the track when I got there, I would not leave until they left. Sometimes, it meant walking 6 or 7 laps but I never lost a battle. It was important that I moved my arms while walking in order to work out my upper body. I played games with that. I named all the different moves I did with my arms. The "toy soldier" was moving them like a toy soldier as I walked. The "boxer" was bringing my arms up and down in front of me with my fists clinched. The "ref" was rotating my arms like a basketball ref making a traveling call. There were others. I looked like a fool. I didn't care. This was my life. I decided not to be fat anymore and if it takes looking like a fool at the park, so be it.

Many weeks went by and I never failed to walk 25 miles. Some days, I only walked 3 miles and other days 7, but when the week was done, I had completed at least 25 miles. While I played games as I walked, walking itself was no game. It was serious and had become my way of life. I was the walking fool. The weight was falling off.

My theme became: Do it today, repeat it tomorrow and the next day and let time become your friend. What if I only lose one pound a week? 52 pounds in a year would be great. It is all about never giving up.

As the days and weeks flew by, it seemed as though my body was getting used to walking. I decided to jog a little in order to get my heart rate up. I jogged from here to the end of the fence. Every time out, I increased the jogging distance. Then, one day, it happened. I jogged a whole mile. Wow! I became emotional thinking about the accomplishment. A whole mile.

I continued to increase the jogging distance. In November of 2009, I entered my very first 5k. I had no clue what a 5k was but my daughter, Tiffany, and I did a 5k in Canton, Georgia on Thanksgiving morning. (A 5k is 3.1 miles.) I jogged about half of it and had a finish time of about 38 minutes. I had no idea about finish times and what was expected. My walking time for a mile was 15 minutes and thought that 40 minutes would be good. Regardless of the time, I finished a 5k race. I won third place in my age division. I know, there were only three of us competing in my division, but I still won a medal. I loved the atmosphere of this running event. It was for a great cause, people were excited, there were bananas and sports drinks and prizes. People were excited about medals and finish times. This event was a life changer for me. I couldn't wait to sign up for another event.

It had been a long time since I had competed in sports and this was exhilarating. I had to do it again and I did.

Along with all of the walking and jogging, I almost forgot.....I was losing weight. My weigh-in routine was every day when I got home from walking. From the time I got off the cruise ship in March 2009 until July 4, 2010, when I ran the Peachtree 10K Road Race (a 10k is 6.2 miles.) in Atlanta, I lost 110 pounds. That is 141 pounds from my peak weight of 333. I lost a whole person.

Walking, then gradually converting to running 25 miles a week along with healthy eating was a winning formula for me. It is a lifestyle I will maintain the rest of my life as long as I can physically run. I love it.

5 DISGUSTED

I lived many frustrating years of being overweight. There are way too many stories to tell about those frustrations. I couldn't begin to remember them all because the frustrations happened most every day of my adult life. I was embarrassed and disgusted, but evidently not enough. After many diets, I had reached a point in my life of total disgust. It was that disgust that brought me to a crisis moment.

Merriam-Webster dictionary says that *disgust* is: "marked aversion aroused by something highly distasteful." An aversion is the act of turning away.

Before I was able to make the decision to change my life, I was disgusted with myself. Being disgusted is actually necessary in the process of change. I can think of many things that disgust me. The abuse of a child, for example. Hypocrisy disgusts me. The problem with many of the things that disgust me, however, is that in most cases, there is nothing I can do to change the situation.

Most of the time, I try to ignore it or turn away as the definition suggests. I may write an e-mail to the editor or send a complaint to the president of a company responsible for whatever disgusted me. That only makes me feel better temporarily but doesn't really change the issue in most cases.

As the years went by and my weight increased, I felt the need to lose weight from time to time. I was successful many times but the success was temporary. A diet is a battle. Many times battles are won even though the war is lost. I tried various approaches to losing weight. I found that every diet worked if I followed the diet plan. Once the diet was over, I returned to my previous life. After all, I loved food. The problem with every diet I did was that I was never disgusted with myself enough to make a lifetime change. I knew that I needed to lose weight but there was never a true disgust with myself. I am convinced that in order for one to make a change in life, there has to be a disgust with the current situation.

A single event can cause a disgust so great that it forces a change. I remember sitting on side of the bed while getting dressed for church. I looked down at my shirt and the buttons were about to pop off. I remember thinking "I am tired of this." I was disgusted with myself. This feeling didn't leave me until I decided to make a change in my life. I was disgusted.

The disgust I am talking about is not the kind where you look away and do nothing. It is true disgust. If I am disgusted with myself, what do others think of me? I knew that people talked about me. I knew that they made fun of me. Children made comments about my weight. While others will talk behind your back, children will just tell you what they think. They call it like they see it. They saw a fat man when they saw me. It was embarrassing to live a life knowing that people were making fun of me behind my back. How could I continue to live like that?

Again, I believe that true disgust must occur before one can make a decision to change. Without disgust, it is easy to return to the previous lifestyle. My disgust was much more than the way I looked. My disgust happened because I realized it was now a health issue. I was a year older than my Dad when he passed away with diabetes at age 53. What made me think I could live a long life being over 300 pounds? After all, I didn't know very many 70 year old 300 pound people. That was only 16 years away for me at that time. I wanted to live longer than that but knew that at 300 pounds, I would not make it. How did I get here? I am disgusted with myself. Disgust was the key to my decision.

In a way, disgust can be a wonderful thing. Without being disgusted I may still be overweight. Jim Rohn says that the day you "had it" can be the most wonderful day of your life.

It is the day you are finally disgusted to the point you will do most anything to change. When you hit the bottom, there is only one direction to go. I lived the day that changed my life. It was a wonderful day. July 16, 2009. By the end of that day, I had realized my disgust, experienced a crisis moment and made a decision to change my life forever. I will never be fat again. What a day that was. What about you? You can do it too.

6 DECISIONS

We make decisions every day. Some decisions are not important at all but must be made. It may be as simple as what pair of pajamas to wear. Even though it doesn't take much thought and is unimportant, it does take a decision. It could be that you need a warmer top tonight, so you look for that long sleeve pajama top. I am reminded of an episode of *All in the Family* in which Archie and Michael had a debate over how to put socks and shoes on. Archie said that normal people put their socks on first, followed by their shoes. Michael argued that you are supposed to put on a sock followed by a shoe and then the other sock followed by a shoe. If you remember the show, Archie and Michael, known as the "Meathead," never came to an agreement on much and this was no different. A decision was made for each of them how to put on shoes and socks.

In the church culture, we grew up hearing about making decisions. Billy Graham was known for his great television crusades but also had a radio broadcast called *The Hour of Decision.* The goal of the program was to persuade listeners that they were in need of a savior and Jesus Christ fulfills that need based on His work on the cross. By the end of the program, it was Dr. Graham's hope that the listener would come to a decision for Christ. We were familiar with this term in our church culture, in fact, we sang a song called *I Have Decided to Follow Jesus.* We were taught that making a decision for Christ would ensure our eternal destiny with Him and others who had made the same decision. That would be an important decision.

There are important decisions and unimportant decisions through life each day. There are also decisions that we make that are not important at the time, but turn out to be a life changing one. When I was 17, my cousin, Skip Davis, called me and asked me to go to a softball game with him. I had other plans and decided not go with him. Really, it was an unimportant decision at the time. Later that night, we got a call that Skip had been killed in a car accident along with 4 other boys. The decision I made may have saved my life. Then again, as I have often wondered, had I been there, would things have been different and the accident not happened? Who knows, but life changing decisions were made that seemed unimportant at the time.

I have made many decisions in my life. Some of them turned out to be great. Some of them didn't turn out as well. Others turned out badly. Hopefully, when I made a decision, one of two things happened; I either made a great decision or I learned something. I believe we learn more by our failures than we do our successes. We have all heard the Thomas Edison quote "I have not failed. I've just found 10,000 ways that won't work." We either have success or we learn from our attempts.

I have made decisions many times to lose weight like most of you. Most of the time, when I decided to lose weight, I did. My mistake, though, was that I made the wrong decision each time. Each time, it was to lose weight. Sure, I would make a goal of losing 30 pounds or 50 pounds and reached the goal. But, you know what happened after that? That's right, I gained it back. Don't judge me, you have done the same. Most every time, we gained it all back. Sometimes, we gained it all back plus a few more pounds. All we do is frustrate ourselves and gain it back. Diets. I hate them and so do you.

I believe that when we experience a crisis moment that causes us to make a decision for healthy living, it is life changing and our minds become renewed through this transformation. It is the difference between going on a diet and becoming a different person. The health related decisions we make can be the difference between enjoying our grandchildren and our grandchildren only seeing pictures and hearing stories about us. I decided that I want to enjoy my grandchildren. When I made the decision to change my life on July 16, 2009, what made that decision successful? What was different this time? It was several things. After living the day that changed my life, I made the decision that I was not going to be fat again. I was done with not being able to bend over to tie my shoes without running out of breath. I was done with looking down at my shirt and realizing that my buttons were about to pop. I was done with putting on a pair of jeans and not being able to snap them together. I was sick of being fat. I wanted to know what it was like to live as a normal person with a normal weight. I was done.

Have you ever had a "done" experience before? Maybe you had a bad experience with a particular company and declared....I'll never buy from that company again. I am done with them. You kept your promise. Not only did you never buy from them again, you told all your friends about your experience. You made a decision. You were done. That's what happened to me. I made the decision to not be fat again. The flaw I had always made concerning losing weight was that my decision was the wrong decision. I had always decided to go on a diet. I decided to lose weight. While those are good decisions, they never worked for me long range. This time, I decided that I was not going to be fat again and was going to live a healthy life.

Another decision that I made was to be healthy. That was a different thought for me. I never thought about that before. I always wanted to go on a diet and lose weight.

This time, I wanted to be healthy and I was going to change my life and be healthy. Many years ago, I heard a story that a minister told. He said that a man and his wife were in an upstairs room of their house during a driving rain storm. They were upstairs to escape the flood waters that was slowly rising. The lady looked outside and saw a hat moving back and forth next door. She asked her husband "what in the world is that?" He answered "that's old Joe. He said he was going to mow the lawn today come hell or high water." That was the kind of decision I made. I was going to be healthy come hell or high water. I had decided.

The number one reason that I am not fat today is that I decided that I was not going to be fat. I know it's not the story you are looking for. You were looking for the magical formula to losing weight. Most people would be happy to pay for it. I'm telling you that decision is the formula. It is the first step to being healthy. In fact, you can't lose weight and be healthy without this decision. For me, Romans 12:2 says it best:

Do not conform to the pattern of this world, but be transformed by the renewing of your mind. Then you will be able to test and approve what God's will is—his good, pleasing and perfect will.

Once I made the decision that I was not going to be fat and that I was going to be healthy, my mind was renewed. I was transformed. I was changed, never to be the same. This decision caused a transformation in me that I can't fully describe. If you are a Christian, you remember the time that you made the decision to follow Christ and make Him the Lord of your life. In that decision, all things became new. You were a new creation. Your mind had been transformed. It was renewed. You were born again.

That experience, though much more important, is very similar to the decision I made to be healthy and to not be fat again. As a result, my journey was easy. Yes, I said it. When talking to people about my weight loss experience, I am asked often "I bet that was hard." Honestly, it was easy once my mind was renewed and I had been transformed. I can't explain the transformation any more than you can explain how your mind was renewed once you decided to follow Christ. It is a new life, but it began with a decision.

7 IT ONLY TAKES ONE TO TANGO

"Just do it." That is the NIKE advertising theme. I have seen it on t-shirts and have heard people use the term when responding to various questions. I heard this way before NIKE used it. Art Williams, founder of A.L. Williams/Primerica, said it often when motivating his sales reps. My wife, Cathy, and I have been involved with A.L. Williams/Primerica since 1988 in several different ways and love the company. When people told Art how great they were going to be in the business, Art would respond with "just do it." In fact, Art has a whole "Do It" speech that is highly motivational. So, "just do it" has been in our vocabulary for a very long time. The problem was, when it came to living a healthy lifestyle, I didn't just do it.

In most activities in life, especially those that involve selling, it takes two to tango. It takes one to sell the product and another to purchase the product. This is the challenge with any sales position.

Regardless of how wonderful the product may be, somebody has to buy it for you to become a successful salesperson. You may have heard the term "he could sell icicles to Eskimos." It is my firm belief that it still takes an Eskimo to purchase the icicle. Good luck with that. I have been involved in a couple of organizations that I was absolutely positive that I would be successful. No matter how excited I was about it, others were not. It is hard to succeed in sales when there is no buyer. You can't force people buy your product. It takes two to tango.

When it comes to living a healthy lifestyle, I have great news. One can tango. I was highly successful with my lifestyle change without having to depend on others. It helps when you have a spouse or a buddy who is on the same program, but it is not necessary to be successful. Back in 1999, Cathy and I lost a ton of weight together doing the Atkins Diet, as did a lot of other people when the Atkins Diet was all the rage. I lost 80 pounds on Atkins and Cathy lost 50. It was easier to lose together because of food preparation but I learned that it is possible to do without a partner. With this new transformation in my life, I had to do it alone and I did. I experienced this transformation through the renewing of my mind. Are you looking for the secret? That is it. It is found in Romans 12:2. I need no help from others to live a healthy lifestyle. That is my story. I did it by myself. I didn't need anyone to buy my product to make the sell. I wish the business world were like that. I would be rich.

I have observed many people on diets. One theme among my friends is their proclamations of God helping them. "If God will help me, I can lose weight." "Oh, God, help me to lose this weight." I have also prayed this prayer many times. I heard my Daddy pray that prayer many times. I grew up on that prayer. It was the prayer we prayed after each meal. We started every diet "in the morning."

After my transition, I realized that God was not going to do this for me; this would not be a case of cosmic liposuction. He gave me the strength, but I had to do it. He enabled me, but I had to do it. He gave me the knowledge, but I had to do it. He gave me the desire, but I had to do it. There are just some things that He expects me to do on my own. He commands me to love my neighbor. He even commands that I love my enemy. He commands and expects me to do it. He does not do it for me. He commands me to turn the other cheek, take care of the widows, feed the hungry and do good to those who persecute me. He does not do it for me. What would be the point? I am not His robot. He wants me to love Him with all my heart, mind, soul and strength. *All my strength.* He does not do it for me but here is the good news. I can do it or He wouldn't have commanded it. He will not force me do it. If I don't do it, He would rather command something inanimate, like a rock, do it. He said, in the book of Luke, that He will cause the rocks to cry out if we didn't praise Him. Isn't it interesting that He won't cause us to praise Him instead of a rock? He doesn't invade our free will.

Just do it. I am not going to sit by and watch the rocks do it. I choose to do it. The great news is that you can too. It only takes one to tango. You do not have to depend on a buyer. Once you have reached the point of disgust and make the decision that you are going to change your life, just do it. God is not going to do it for you. You do it. What holds you back? What ever it is, defeat it. Just do it. Start today, not in the morning.

8 OVERCOMING THE MIND

There have been many books written and seminars held that focused on the subject of overcoming the mind. Motivational speakers and authors have made millions of dollars on the subject, yet, it remains the number one obstacle of reaching our goals. I have learned through my experience that overcoming the mind is the key component to my weight loss and running success. I wrote a blog concerning a particular experience called "I Left the Devil at Mile Marker 2." I want to be clear about something, however. I don't literally mean Satan. Without getting into a long theological discussion, the devil is not omni-present like God, so I have never come in contact with the devil. Sure, I have come in contact with *a* devil but never *the* devil. So, in this blog, "the devil" is really my mind. **Here is the blog:**

Today was my "long run" day. In my marathon training, one day a week is designated as the long run of the week. Today was that day. My goal was 13 miles.

I had an unexpected guest in today's run. The devil. He ran with me for 2 miles. He is not an encourager. In fact, he fed my mind with discouraging thoughts.

"You can't run more than 4 miles today. Your leg is hurting and you're going to really mess it up. There is a storm coming and you're going to get caught in it so you better quit now. You just ran the Peachtree and need to be resting. What makes you think you can run a marathon anyway? You are going to embarrass yourself. Wouldn't a milkshake taste good right about now? You're going to need to go to the bathroom before you finish. You didn't have coffee and you're going to get a headache. Your stomach is hurting. You shouldn't be wearing those old shoes."

The devil is really a talker and talked to me for two miles. I almost gave in and quit. I thought about all of those things he was saying to me. He had some good points, but, he got tired at mile marker 2 and I ran off and left him. It was a great run after that. I thought about why I was training for a marathon. I thought about my friends. All of the motivating things that have been said to me over the last several months. I ran 13.06 miles today. When I got back to mile marker 2 on my way back, the devil had packed up and gone home. He was defeated and I won today. Maybe next week, he'll just stay home because he can't even run 2 miles. Somewhere, I hear the song "the devil went down to Georgia."

I have heard it said by runners such as Jeff Galloway that running is a mental sport. I have found that to be true. If I can overcome the mind, I have won most of the battle.

Overcoming the mind means renewing your mind. To renew is to start over. The mind becomes new. The old things no longer control your mind. The mind is overcome. I am no longer a fat man. It is not a part of my life. I overcame my mind and it has been transformed. I am changed. I am transformed. The mind can be overcome. The mind must be overcome. You can do it too.

9 THE FOOD CULTURE

Since I have lived most of my life being overweight, I am an expert on how to lose and how to gain weight. Most of you already know how to lose and gain weight, but let's review.

If you follow a diet, you will lose weight. If all you want to do is simply drop a few pounds, go on a diet. If you are obese, a diet is only placing a bandaid over a more serious problem. Sure, you'll lose some weight but you know what happens later. We always gain it back. Spiritually speaking, we can follow every commandment but unless we are a believer in Jesus, we do not secure eternal life with Christ. I believe that you must change you first or it is only a temporary fix.

I have always heard that in order to plan for the future you must understand where you have been. Remembering your history helps you to not repeat your mistakes. There are some things we just don't want to remember but it is essential to changing our direction.

It was pretty easy for me to realize how I let myself get to 333 pounds. I am a product of several cultures that are surrounded by food. Let's take a look at some of those cultures.

It is no mystery why Southerners lead the nation in obesity. It all begins with Southern cuisine. The South is known for its fried chicken, biscuits, gravy, apple and peach pies. We are known for great sweet tea. Paula Deen is our queen. The list of fattening Southern food is very long. It's not only what we eat but how we prepare it and when we eat it. Fried everything. Even our "healthy" green beans are seasoned with ham. It's just how we do it.

Most everybody in the South knows how Mama or Grandma can make biscuits and gravy. Not just any gravy but sausage gravy. Of course, you have to add butter and homemade jam. Breakfast is not complete without eggs and bacon or ham. We know how to get the day started. It used to make sense when most people worked a physical job like farming all day. Not these days for most of us, however. We felt we had no choice but to eat. What about those starving children in foreign countries, as Mama compelled us to clean our plates?

Adding to our great Southern food is our "Southern hospitality." Y'all come eat with us. This means not only do we eat Mama's food, we're always invited to eat your Mama's food as well. Southerners are always eager to feed you. We are a fellowshipping bunch. Nothing gets thrown away either. We eat until it's all gone or it is served tomorrow with more biscuits and gravy. Southerners love good, fattening food.

At school, we were rewarded for cleaning our plates. What was the reward? Another hot bread roll. I don't know why, but schools had the best rolls. I remember "Maybelle's rolls" at Roswell High School. Sometimes it meant that you had to hide the green peas or carrots to get another roll. I did that many times. It was always great to find a friend who liked broccoli.

In the South, we love our food. We worship our food almost as much as football. We love to share our food. It is our culture. My Mom and Dad grew up in the South during the Great Depression and did what they had to do to survive. That included foods that were not as healthy. My Dad's favorite meal was cornbread in buttermilk. I never attempted that. They ate it all and threw away nothing.

I grew up in another culture that was food driven: The church culture. Church folks love to eat as well. Every fellowship is surrounded by food. The most important discussion while driving to church on Sunday morning is where to eat after church. That was a big deal. I understand it. It is a time of enjoying good company while we eat. It was fun but not always healthy.

Growing up in a strict religious environment, we were not allowed to do much in the way of entertainment other than going out to eat. There was nothing like eating pizza after church on Sunday night with your friends. It was our culture. We didn't realize what a bad precedent it was setting for our lives.

I had another disadvantage. I lived in the home of a preacher. People liked to feed us. Not only would they feed us but they would make their favorite dessert dish for us. Usually, it was 2 or 3 desserts. If we had peach cobbler, we had to have ice cream as well. When folks go to the trouble of making a cake, you have to eat it and we did. A second helping was a requirement. Not only was my Dad the preacher, he worked a job in Atlanta as a bread delivery man. Later, he owned his business selling cakes, pies and other goodies. Of course, he always brought home some of those goodies. He never actually ate any of these goodies, he just wanted to "try" a piece. My Dad was a funny man. I wish he had taken care of himself.

This lifestyle was not conducive to healthy living. My Mother really tried. She was not overweight and knew that it was bad for us. She fought a losing battle trying to get us to eat healthy. I didn't listen and my Dad didn't either. As a result, my Dad died at age 53 with diabetes. You would think that I would have learned a lesson. I didn't. The culture I grew up in was rooted deep inside of me and it took it's toll. Sadly, it controlled my life for too many years. It controls many other people as well. When I attend church functions, it is very sad to see so many obese people. I hope that one day, they will live the day that changes their life and make the dramatic change I was able to make.

Another culture that affects us is the fast food culture. This one may be our biggest downfall. I really don't need to go into much detail with this one as I believe we are all aware of the dangers of eating a double cheeseburger, a large order of fries and a chocolate milkshake for dinner. When I was on the road working in photography, I was a frequent visitor.

In order to change my life, I had to reject these food cultures and overcome my mind. I did it and so can you.

10 HEALED

Many times in my life, I have experienced answered prayers. It didn't always turn out like I thought I wanted at the time, but God has been good to me and my family. I can't write about my experience without sharing this story of healing because it is significant to my story. Growing up in the church, one of my favorite activities was church league softball. It really began in Georgia Church of God Youth Camp at the old Camp Ground on Buford Highway in Doraville, Georgia. Softball was so important to my buddies and me that we actually recruited good players to be in our youth camp room the following year. We lived for youth camp softball. After my Dad passed away, I attended Doraville Church of God and played many softball games. I was a pitcher and took great pride in playing the position. Over the years, I took several line drives back up the middle that hit my foot. Even though I was overweight, I had pretty quick reflexes but sometimes I would get nailed by a line drive.

At the time, it didn't seem serious. Years later, in the early 1980s, my right foot began to give me trouble. It felt much like a sprained ankle and it was difficult to walk without pain. I went to the podiatrist to have it checked out. He said that I had several bone spurs on top of my right foot, probably from being hit while playing softball. He told me that the pain would gradually get worse and that eventually, it would be so bad that I wouldn't be able to walk. It looked as though surgery was necessary. In fact, it was so bad that the doctor wanted to send me to someone with more experience as he had never seen one that bad. How comforting. The only surgery I have ever had was when I was 6 weeks old and fortunately, can't remember that.

While contemplating surgery, Doraville Church of God began a revival meeting. This was when Robert Herrin was the pastor, over 25 years ago. One night at the revival, the minister had a healing line. If you grew up in this type of church, you know what I'm talking about. Our church taught and believed in divine healing. I saw many people healed through the years. One night during the revival, the minister said "if anybody here has a physical need, come forward for prayer." I didn't have to think about it long while sitting there in pain. I went to the altar for prayer along with many other people. He prayed for my foot and I felt a warm feeling go through it much like I have heard others describe during a healing. I looked at my foot and the bone spur was still there but it felt some better. As the days went by, my foot did not hurt as bad. Eventually, I forgot about it. It was healed. No surgery for me.

That was over 25 years ago and the bone spurs can still be seen. I'll show them to you if you want to see them. It has not hurt even once since that time. Not only am I still walking on it without pain, I am a runner. Thank you, Lord, for healing. Why are the bone spurs still there? I guess to remind me. In fact, it lends credibility to my story when sharing it with others. God is just like that.

11 THE PEACHTREE ROAD RACE

I began my quest to run the Peachtree Road Race by continuing to train. I was excited to give this a try. **I wrote a blog about my first Peachtree experience:**

I finally did it. I ran the Peachtree Road Race on July 4, 2010 at the weight of 192. I failed to make it to my goal of 190 but who's counting? My original goal was 190 by my birthday, December 27, 2010. When I began this journey last year to lose the weight, my friend, Jeff Thomas, challenged me to make the Peachtree Road Race a goal. Not wanting to be one who backs off of a good "double dog dare," I took up the challenge. After I began walking seriously, in order to get my heart rate up, I jogged a little. I jogged more and more and my jogging became habit forming and enjoyable. Go figure. My first real victory jogging was when I jogged a whole mile without having to walk. My next victory was running a 5k in Buford, Georgia straight through without having to walk. I was ready for the Peachtree.

My friend, Jeff Thomas, has run the Peachtree 31 years in a row. He knows the ropes and that really helped me. I have this anxiety thing about doing new things and having Jeff there helped ease my anxieties. We met at the MARTA train station in Doraville at 5:30 A.M. The early time was my idea and Jeff gave in, realizing my anxiety. That's what friends are for. We got to the Lenox station and hung out until race time. It was some of the best people watching I had ever done. You name it and it was running. There was everybody from Little Bo Peep to Uncle Sam.

Where's the bathroom? Oh, they did a great job, pardon the pun. There were Job Johnnies, Port-a-Potties, or whatever you call them, everywhere. Thank God, one of my anxieties was taken care of. I even skipped my coffee to make sure I didn't need to pee while running down Peachtree Street. I bet there were 100 potties with 30 people standing in line for each one. When I saw that, I suddenly needed to pee again. So, we got in line. The line was so bad that once I went, I got back in line.

Anticipating the start, people lined up from Phipps Plaza to Lenox Square, the start line. Each person had a number with a letter that corresponded with their anticipated finish time.

Everyone with the letter "A" was in the front of the line, after the elite runners. Next, was everyone with a "B" and so forth. I had an "L" but ran with Jeff who had an "M." Pastor Jeff Henderson of Buckhead Church, a North Point campus, did the prayer, which was cool.

Here we are watching each wave before ours take off. 55,000 of our closest friends running the Peachtree. What an exciting time. While waiting, I reflected on my journey of losing weight over the last year. The title of this blog is "From 333 to the Peachtree" because my peak weight several years ago was 333 pounds. Here I am 141 pounds later about to run the Peachtree. I was imagining having to run with a 141 pound weight on my shoulder. What an amazing feeling I wish my fellow overweight friends could feel. At 8:23, we're off! One of the surprising things to me about the Peachtree was the number of people that had no interest in running. Too many walkers in this race. That's because the Peachtree is not a race for those behind the "D" runners. It is an event, not a competition. I hung with Jeff. Again, it's an event, not a competition, so we enjoyed the sites. There were many sites along the way. My favorite was passing the Shepherd Center. The street was lined with folks in wheelchairs cheering those of us who could run. As I passed, I waved and clapped for them. Former Senator Max Cleland, disabled Viet Nam veteran was there. While I don't care for his politics, I honor his service to this country. It was pretty cool passing him as he was clapping for us.

Another person I saw was Willorene Morrow. Out of all the people standing on the sidelines, she was the only person I recognized. I have known this great lady since 1987. I met Willie in Warner Robins at an A.L. Williams meeting. Her son is Duane Morrow. He is one of my heroes and an inspiration to many.

At about the 4 mile marker, Jeff told me to run the rest of the way and he would meet me back at Piedmont Park, where the race finishes. So, I took off. Man, this was fun. I enjoyed the finish. I had a sense of accomplishment as I ran down the final hill with the finish line in front of me. Mark 12:30-31 has been my theme during this weight loss journey and it was on my mind as I ran toward the finish line. In fact, I had a t-shirt with "Mark 12:30-31" printed on the back. I want to love the Lord with all my strength. I crossed the finish line with a 1:18:19 time. I beat about 24,000 runners. (I know, there were 55,000 running) Last year, I couldn't run to the mailbox and back. Like the Apostle Paul, I ran the race and I finished the course. There laid before me was a t-shirt. I wonder what kind of finish time Paul would have at the Peachtree Road Race?

Where's my t-shirt? After crossing the finish line, the crowd is in Piedmont Park. Lots of goodies, people on cell phones, some needing medical attention but all getting their prize, a Peachtree Road Race t-shirt. My mind still wants to get a 3XL t-shirt, but I wear a large now. I got my t-shirt. I met Jeff at our designated spot. We ran into Anita Livingston Rudzinski, who is an avid runner and fellow Church of God PK. We visited a bit and then made the next trip of our journey, back to the MARTA station. What a zoo that was, but, we made it back and the goal was complete. One final thing, my coffee. A trip to Starbucks made the day complete. Just don't spill coffee on my new t-shirt.

A year later, I ran the Peachtree Road Race again. Here is my blog about that experience:

There were about 60,000 runners. I beat around 42,000 runners at the Peachtree Road Race in Atlanta, the world's largest 10k. In 2010, I ran my first Peachtree. My friend, Jeff Thomas, showed me the ropes. I was intimidated by it all. My time was a little over 1:18. It was fun and I knew I wanted to do it again. This year, I was more experienced and had greater expectations for my run. I had a few challenges, however. Most runners do, so there are no excuses. My time was 1:04:34 this year. My goal was to break 1:00 but it wasn't meant to be this time and remains a goal of mine.

I have been battling a leg injury over the last couple of weeks. It felt much better today but it was a little painful. The temperature and humidity were higher than last year. Cardiac Hill seemed much longer this year with the heat. I could really tell a difference. I walked some while drinking water. Last year, the folks spraying water on the runners seemed a bit annoying to me. Not this year. I embraced every drop that was slung my way. When I got a cup of water, half of it went on my bald head. It felt refreshing.

I love seeing the people along the way. It is a great place to people watch. I even saw some familiar faces. My lifelong friend, Denny Pritchett and his wife, Beth, Robert Daugherty and Philip Bray. Also, seeing Anita Livingston Rudzinski again at the beginning of the race was nice too. The kids slapping "high fives" and "fist pumps" was pretty cool as well. There were bands playing all along the way. I know, I was listening to my music, but it was still nice to see them. There were a couple of guys running in the race carrying a huge American flag. I loved it.

Some advantages I had this year was qualifying for a better "wave" time. I qualified for the "D" wave. That meant that I got to start earlier with cooler temperatures than if I had an "L" like last year. There were no walkers in front of me and not as many people to follow. What difference does that make? Body heat and lots of it.

After the race, we emptied into Piedmont Park for t-shirt pickup, water and fruit. Then, I walked 1 1/2 miles to the North Avenue MARTA Station for the trip back north.

I have competed, and I use that word loosely, in two Peachtree Road Races. I look forward to it being an annual tradition and running it in under an hour. Why not join me?

12 RUNNING A MARATHON

After proclaiming to my friends that I would never run a marathon, I had a change of heart. Maybe it was just heartburn. I decided to run a marathon. Here is my blog concerning the announcement:

I have Decided to Run the Chicago Marathon

I have gone and done it now. I have committed to running a marathon. After completing a half marathon at Disney World in January 2011, a full marathon is the next step. I have been searching for a marathon over the last couple of months and have decided on the Chicago Marathon. The course in Chicago is flat. That's a good thing. The marathon is on October 9, 2011. The weather should be nice and cool. It adds to my goal of running in different states, giving me Illinois. In order to get into the Chicago, I had to choose a charity to run with and fund raise for. It was a very easy choice for me. I will be running for the Alzheimer's Association in honor of my father-in-law, Dr. Charles W. Conn. All of the pieces are falling together. I wish he could see me now. I believe he would be proud of me.

I am registered and it's all set. Tiffany is also running the Chicago Marathon. She has chosen Girls on the Run, an organization that educates and prepares preteen girls for a lifetime of self respect and healthy living. Cathy will make the trip to Chicago with us. We are working on those plans. Our fundraising efforts do not include any of our personal expenses. All donations go directly to the charities, so if you contribute, you are only donating to the charity. Donations are tax deductible. Also, if you donate in the name of a loved one, I will have their name somewhere on me. I haven't decided yet but I will either have their names written on a hat or my shirt. Thank you so much for considering a donation. The cause is great and we all are vulnerable to this disease.

Now, it is time to begin training. My running routine has been 5.5 miles several times a week at Big Creek Greenway in Forsyth County. My goal is to increase that to 6.2, which is a 10k. Once a week, I will stretch that. On May 8, I ran 8 miles. My goal is to increase that each week and eventually run 20 miles by sometime in September. Let the training begin. I will accept any suggestions from those of you have been through this process.

Here are my notes on training for the Chicago Marathon:

Training for the Chicago Marathon on October 9. One long run per week. I will try to post each week.

05/08 - 8 miles at BCG (Big Creek Greenway)

Story: I had a rock in my shoe right at the beginning and stopped to remove it. While I was removing the rock, a couple ending their run, came by. The gentleman was wearing a Chicago Marathon shirt so I stopped him and talked to him about it. He said it is a great marathon, flat, cool and people all along the route cheering for you. He liked it so much he is doing it again this year. That was an incredible moment of confirmation for me. He did not know that I was having doubts about running the Chicago and that God had sent him my way. Thanks Chris and Erica.

05/19 - On this weekend, Cathy and I are going to Denver, Colorado and driving up to South Dakota, North Dakota, Nebraska and Wyoming. The purpose is to complete my visit to 50 states. On 5/21, I will be running a 5k in Spearfish, South Dakota. (Note: weather conditions canceled this run) It is a trail run so my time will not be good. My long run for this weekend won't happen until Tuesday or Wednesday when we return.

05/24 - Ran 9.3 miles on the Greenway today. The temp got to 80 and I went without taking water so I slowed way down. I walked more than I wanted to. I was afraid of dehydration. Still got in 9.3. My weight was down to 200.5. It was 207 when I got up. I lost a lot of water. Lesson learned.

6/2 - Did my long run today. I did 10 miles with very little walking. Probably only 2/10 of a mile. I got out before it got too hot, though it was almost 80 when I finished. I felt pretty good about the run today. My weight was at 204.5.

6/8 - Went to Big Creek Greenway and ran from the Bethelview trailhead to Georgia 400. That is 11.1 miles. I ran it in 132 minutes which is about a 12 minute mile. I only walked about 2/10 of a mile after the heat was getting to me a bit. It was 72 when I started and 80 when I finished. My weight was 202.5 after this run. I did not run for 2 days before the long run.

6/15 - Long run day once again. I was geared up to run after taking 2 days off. My left hip has been aching just a bit. I did 11.6 miles at Big Creek Greenway. That is from Bethelview to the 1 mile marker just before McFarland. The whole Greenway is 13.6 miles. This was the third longest run I have done. I ran most of the way until something happened at around mile 8. One of the planks on the boardwalk was raised a bit and I tripped. When I caught my balance, I jammed the same hip that was already aching. I slowed way down and eventually had to walk the last mile. One of my fears is that something like this will happen just before the Chicago. Accidents happen and I have to think positive.

6/23 - No long run this week. I am nursing this crazy leg injury. I did a 5k in Suwanee, GA on Saturday and came in at 27:15 which wasn't bad considering the small hills and the leg injury.

6/29 - I made it to 12.1 miles today. I still have pain in my left leg but survived the run. I walked probably about 1 1/2 miles of the run. On 6/30, I had my annual physical. I had x-rays done on my hip. Dr. Morrow recommends physical therapy. I am thinking that through. My weight was up to 204 as a result of not running as much this past week. Next up, the Peachtree Road Race.

7/06 - I survived 13.06 miles today. I ran the Peachtree 2 days earlier at 64:34, which wasn't too bad considering the heat and humidity. Cardiac Hill was especially rough. Been there and got the t-shirt. As for today's run, I wasn't mentally ready. The first 2 miles was really rough. I walked some but that is the plan. I won't be running a full marathon without walking some. My weight was at 204. I'm not losing weight and that is a concern. I have to make a better effort to drop some weight. I really need to be around 190 come marathon time. All of my numbers from last week's physical came in great.

7/14 - It has been HOT here all week. I did an 8 mile run in 80 degree temps and 90% humidity. I am counting that as my long run this week. I know...it's cheating, but it is too hot and too humid to attempt anything longer. We went to Cincinnati and I ran with Tiffany on Saturday morning. We did a 3.2 mile run. The weather was nice.

7/18 - I did my longest run ever today. 13.63 miles. That is the Big Creek Greenway from Bethleview to McFarland Rd and back. Today was supposed to be the coolest day of the week, so I ran today even though it's Monday. My weight was 200.5 today. Going for 14 miles next week. The long runs have begun.

7/29 - It's been a while but I did my long run today. 14.2 miles. I averaged 12:29 per mile. I would be happy with that in the marathon. That would be about a 5:30 finish. My goal is to finish, of course, but a time under 6 hours would be a bonus. Chicago will be cooler and a lower altitude plus the cheering fans along the way will motivate me. It's 10 weeks until marathon time.

8/5 - Long run day. I did 15.2 on the Greenway. I got started at 7AM and it was still 72 degrees. By the time I got back to the pasture, 2 1/2 miles from the finish, it was 80. It is really tough running in 80 degrees with the sun blasting you after you have run 12 miles. But, I survived.

I took 2 Coconut waters and 3 Power Gels with me. I averaged 12:46 per mile which wasn't too bad. I would take that for the marathon right now. My weight was at 200.5 when I got home. Next week, 16 miles.

8/12 - Today was 16 mile day. I did it. The weather was a little cooler but not much. I did 16.1 miles with an average pace of 12:51. I am staying under 13 minute miles. I would love to be under 13 minute miles for the marathon. I have no clue if I can do it. Today was a good day. Next week, 17 miles.

8/20 - The weather was not cooler today. I made 17 miles at a 12:41 clip, which was better that last week's 16 miles in cooler weather. Not bad. Things are moving along just fine. I used my new fuel belt that holds 4-12 ounce drinks. I ordered Accelerade from GNC and it wasn't bad. I lost my nip guards at the 3 mile mark, which stunk. I have to find another solution because a blistered nip is not fun. Next week, I will do 18 miles then I do 20 miles twice in September.

8/25 - I probably came back too soon to run my long run. It was only 5 days ago that I ran 17, but I did 18.28 today. My pace was 12:57. The heat got to me late and I had to walk more than I really wanted to. I did the usual Big Creek Greenway but went into Fowler Park for the first time to make sure I added to the distance. I found out that it is a good place to get some water and use the bathroom along the way. Also, there is a football field with a running track around it. I did a lap there. I have to do 2 more long runs before the marathon. Both of them 20 miles. I really wish the weather would get cooler.

9/05 - I didn't do a long run last week. I did several runs but I only need to do 2 runs of 20 miles and it is 5 weeks until the marathon. Today, while running, I walked a bit and talked with a man and woman who is walking most every day. I found out he is the head football coach for West Forsyth, Coach Frank Hepler and his wife, Heidi. We had a nice visit talking about working on being fit. I saw Chris, who is also training for the Chicago. He did his 20 mile run today. It is really neat meeting new people on the Greenway. It is supposed to rain over the next 3 days and after that it should be cooler. I will do my 20 miles run sometime over the next week.

9/7 - The weather got cooler so I took advantage and did my 20 mile run. It was 57 and drizzling rain when I started. This is the first time I have been in 50 degree weather in several months and did it ever feel good. I actually did it. I know now that I can do the marathon barring injury. I did 20.1 miles in a 13.22 per mile pace. The pace is not that great, but good enough. I could have walked the remaining 6 miles and made it in about 6 hours. The Chicago allows for a 6:30 finish. I didn't take food today, only 4 Power Gels and 4 containers of Accelerade. I went into Fowler Park and did 4 laps on the track there. I did a couple of backtracks between 400 and McFarland. I saw Chris when I started and he gave me some words of encouragement. I saw Gary today too. New friends are nice. Of course old friends keep me motivated as well. Sometimes, I worry that they get tired of hearing about it. I apologize for that but to be successful, I have to be passionate, obsessed and annoying. I have to do one more 20 mile run and have 3 weeks to do it. It's getting close.

9/16 - No real long run this week, however, Tiffany and I did the whole Big Creek Greenway, which is 13.6 miles. GPS said it was 13.5. We tried a plan. We did a run 2 miles, walk 1 plan. That was interesting. We did it with a 12:07 per mile average. This seems like a great strategy for the marathon. I never got tired and could have walked the remaining 13 miles and finished with about a 13:30 per mile minute. This makes me realize that I can do the marathon barring injury. There are no doubts and the mental part of this is huge. I still have to do another 20 miler. I have less than 3 weeks so I will probably do it in about a week from now. I am getting excited.

9/28 - It's been a while since my last update. Tiffany and I did a 13.5 mile run about 10 days ago. We did run 2, walk 1 and finished with a 12:07 per mile average. I had to travel to Cincinnati and it rained me out. After that, we had Nantahala, our family reunion and I didn't run. I ran 9 miles using the R2W1 method on 9/27. Now, I am sick with a cold. I went to the doctor and got a shot today. I don't think I have time to do another long run since it is only 11 days until the marathon and I am still sick. I am confident about the marathon, however. Tiffany and I will do the R2W1 method and should do fine.

10/1 - I did another 13.5 run today at the Greenway. This time, my time was a little better at a 11:43 pace. When I started, it was the coolest weather since last winter at 46 degrees. I was actually cold. Again, I did the R2W1 method and it worked great. I am sure Tiffany and I will go with this for the marathon. One week from right now, we will be in Chicago getting pumped up for the marathon. It has been a long training time and we are ready to get this thing done. I am so excited to be running in honor of my father-in-law and the other folks who have donated to the cause. 8 more days.

10/6 - The training is all complete. Thankfully, I am injury free and am ready to go. We are leaving in the morning for Cincinnati. We will spend the night with Tiffany and get up early Saturday and head for Chicago. The weather is supposed to be warm. A high of 77 right now, which is way too warm in Chicago this time of year. It is what it is. I figure that it will not affect us as much since we have a goal of finishing and not a certain time in mind. On to Chicago.

13 THE CHICAGO MARATHON

After 5 months of training, the time came for the trip to Chicago for the marathon on October 9, 2011. Cathy and I drove to Cincinnati and spent the night with Tiffany before leaving for Chicago early Saturday morning. Upon our arrival in Chicago, we did a little shopping before going to our hotel, the Embassy Suites. We went to the Chicago Marathon Expo to pick up our packets which included our bib and t-shirt. There was plenty of time to browse around the Expo. There were companies selling their running accessories as well as charities introducing their organizations. Tiffany was representing Girls on the Run and I was representing the Alzheimer's Association. We met with our groups at the Expo. We enjoyed lots of people watching. After we left the Expo, it was time to go back to the hotel and chill. Cathy and Tiffany went out on the town to experience a little bit of Chicago.

On Sunday morning, race day, we were on Central time, helping us a bit. We were up at 5AM.

Race time was 7:30. We got dressed for the race, which included my shirt with names of the donors' loved ones on the back and a picture of *Torch Magazine* with Charles Conn's picture on the front and my lucky green Lee University hat. We made sure we had everything we needed before we left for Grant Park, the starting line. We took the subway for a couple of stops and walked over to the park.

We enjoyed lots of people watching here. There were serious runners and others dressed like it was Halloween. There was a ballerina running next to a serious runner. Too many outfits for me to describe. We arrived in the 12 minute per mile corral and hung out there for more people watching. The sun was beginning to rise over the lake and the sun hitting the skyline was just incredible. As I stood there waiting on the start, I begin to reflect on the training, the folks who graciously donated to the cause, the significance of running with my youngest daughter and the ones I was running for. Most of all, my father-in-law, Charles Conn. He would have been so proud of us. This reflection prepared me for the beginning of the race. I had only done 20 miles at one time and this was 26.2. I was ready.

Time was drawing near to the beginning of the race. There were probably 40,000 people in front of us and 5,000 behind us. Just a mass of people waiting for the race. After the National Anthem, it was race time. The elite runners were off and running as we slowly walked like cattle to the slaughter toward the start line. Lots of music like "Eye of the Tiger" and "We Are the Champions" to pump us up. We hit the start line almost 18 minutes after the race began. We were off.

Without trying to describe all 6 hours of racing through the streets of Chicago, I will hit on the highlights. In the first mile, we passed a gentleman who was at least 80 years old. He was humped over and walking sideways. I told Tiffany "bless his heart, he'll never make it." Our biggest first challenge was to not start too fast. We knew the the temperatures were going into the mid 70s, which is too warm for this. So, a slow beginning was key to our success. We did a good job of going slow and by the time we hit the halfway point, we knew what we had to do to beat 6 hours. We ran two miles, walked one. We did that until the halfway point. While we were walking, guess who passed us? That's right. The gentleman who was humped over with the "blessed heart." He passed us and we never caught up with him. That was an incredible inspiration. Obviously, he had done this before.

We didn't have a time goal but if we had one, it was to be under 6 hours. They allow 6:30. Even though an elderly man who was walking beat us, we didn't want to be the last one to cross the finish line. We were told that 1.7 million people lined the streets cheering for the runners. I believe it. The signs were incredible. Some were as simple as "Go Runners" and many others were specific to a runner friend of theirs. "Go (enter your name)" was nice. Just after the 2 mile marker, I saw "I thought you said 2.62." I liked "Worst Parade Ever" and "Someday you won't be able to do this. Today is not that day." I wish it had been possible to take pictures of all the signs. There is no way I can remember all of them but most were very creative. There were a few x-rated signs as well as inspirational signs. This is Chicago. It was a big time mix just like the people who were cheering.

There was plenty entertainment along the way. My favorite was Elvis. He had a stage about 10 feet high right on the edge of the road and was one of the best I have ever seen. We also saw Lady Gaga. Members of the Moody Bible Church were lined up cheering as Christian music was playing in the background. This was a Sunday morning and it was nice they were out supporting the runners. Through every ethnic neighborhood, there was entertainment. Chinatown was the best. We saw high school cheerleaders and charity clubs cheering as we ran by. I absolutely loved every bit of it. You could not be bored running this marathon.

Cathy came to mile marker 14 to cheer us on. All along the way, we saw people connecting with their loved ones. The streets were full almost the whole way. Lots of people stuck their hands out for "giving five" along the way. The children were so cute trying to slap hands all along the way. This was a big event for the spectators. The marathon organizers did a great job with handing out water and sports drinks. There were stations every mile. A couple of stations had wet sponges which came in handy considering the heat. All along the way, people sprayed water to help us keep cool. That was appreciated as well.

After the half way point, we knew about what our time would be if we walked the rest of the way, so that helped us stay focused on our time. We started off running two, walking one but at about mile 18, we did more run one, walk one. We walked mile markers 23-25 and then ran the rest of the way. You always want to run through the finish line.

We never hit "the wall" using our strategy. It was the best way for us to complete the marathon, which I said all along was my goal. That last mile was amazing. We had left 6 hours earlier from this spot in Grant Park and now, after 26.2 miles through the city of Chicago, we were back at Grant Park. Lots of people cheering and encouraging us to "keep going" and "you're almost there." What a sense of accomplishment to cross the finish line.

I had played this in my mind many times as I trained back on the Big Creek Greenway in Cumming. Every time I played it out in my mind, I was emotional. When I crossed the finish line for real, I wasn't emotional at all. I wanted to rest. My time was 5:54:14. We got our medals and took advantage of some free stuff before meeting Cathy at the "Girls on the Run" table at the Congress Hotel across from Grant Park. I was feeling light-headed again. This happened to me at the Disney Half Marathon. It is a case of my blood pressure going low after my legs stopped, which was pumping blood. I survived. I just finished the Chicago Marathon, a goal I had been training for since May.

Next stop, real Chicago Pizza then back to the room for rest and the trip home on Monday. What an unforgettable experience.

14 THE FOOD STRATEGY

I did not lose weight by exercise alone. In fact, experts say that when losing weight, food intake is much more significant than exercise. Once the weight is lost, exercise is more significant in order to maintain the weight loss. One thing that I found to be true was that exercise enhanced my weight loss in that it affected my metabolism. When I walked or ran, I didn't really feel like eating very much. Others have told me just the opposite so this is not set in stone.

I am now going to share with you what I believe to be the main reason for my success in losing weight as far as food is concerned. Every advertised diet plan bombards you with what you are allowed to eat. Diet plans tell you what time to eat, how much to eat and what types of food to eat. We see commercials with the smiling, thin girl telling us that on her diet, you can enjoy a piece of key lime. Sign me up for the key lime pie diet. She looks pretty good so it must be fine to eat it. We see magazines at the grocery store checkout of celebrities selling their weight loss systems in which you can eat what you want if you will take a pill and lose weight while you sleep. It is a never ending bombardment. It becomes an obsession to the point that all you think about all day is food.

In our food driven culture, it is hard to avoid the temptation of fattening foods. You cannot go through the day without being tempted with food. As I write today, Dunkin' Donuts and Krispy Kreme are offering free donuts. They know that if I go there, I will not have one donut and a glass of water. It happens every day. Buy one, get one free. A free drink with a hamburger and fries. We don't just order a hamburger but a #2 meal upsized. It starts at an early age. A toy with your hamburger and fries. No wonder we are an obese nation. Our culture is one of too much eating and too little exercise. Video games have taken the place of football in the back yard or bike riding in the neighborhood.

I understand the need for groups like Weight Watchers. It has been around a long time and does a great job helping folks lose weight. Some need the support and it really works for those who follow the plan. I know many people who have successfully lost weight through Weight Watchers. There are also fad diets like the Atkins Diet and the South Beach Diet. Again, I have no problem with these. In fact, my doctor recommended the South Beach Diet. I believe that going low carb is a great way for an obese person to lose weight. I lost 80 pounds on the Atkins Diet in 2000. It works if you follow the plan closely. But for me, a diet is a single battle and I am trying to win a war.

Here is my secret: **Forget about food**. That's right, only eat to fuel your body. The bottom line is: Eat a little. Exercise a lot.

The old saying "you should eat to live and not live to eat" is absolutely true and is my main point. I only eat to fuel my body. I am asked all the time "how are you losing the weight, what are you eating?" "How did you do it." Enquiring minds want to know. It is as simple as eat a little and exercise a lot. Of course we have to eat healthy, making sure we get the vitamins and nutrients we need, but it is as simple as cutting back and exercising.

There is no secret other than to just do it. Decide you will and just do it. Do it today. Do it tomorrow and the next day. Repeat this every day and let time become your friend. Time became my friend. A year of healthy living flew by. I never gave up. I didn't cheat. When people asked me to eat something I shouldn't, I simply said "I appreciate the offer but that is not a part of my life anymore." It was important to let people know about my new life. I was a new person. I was not the old Eddie Robbins. Romans 12:2 explains it best. A renewed mind and a transformed life. You can do it too.

15 HOW DO I MAINTAIN?

Throughout my weight loss period, I dreamed of what it would be like to reach my goal. I had visions of eating like a normal 200 pound man, enjoying whatever I wanted. It was a good motivator but it turned out to be unrealistic. I hate to break this to you, but it didn't work that way for me. As I write, I have maintained my weight, in a 10 pound range, for about 18 months. I have no intention of ever going back. There are probably people who think I will gain the weight back. Keep thinking it if you want, but it will not happen.

I am a changed man. Once I got close to my goal, when I ate a little too much, I gained a little weight. It has occurred to me that I will always have to watch the food intake. I can't let myself go for any period of time. I have learned to maintain. It is my life now.

Maintenance is so important to the plan. If you think about it, every diet works if you follow the plan to the letter. We know that most people gain their weight back after they reach their goal. They either gain some, all or even surpass their previous weight. Why is this? In my case, like I have said, I am a changed man. I refuse to go back. I decided and I am sticking to it. I believe the reason people gain it back is not because they quit. After all, they reached the goal. The reason they gain it back is because they never learned how to maintain.

Most of you will have to put this book up and pull it back out after you reach your desired weight. So, let's assume you have lost the weight. Congratulations. If you're a man, how does it feel to be able to cross your legs like a girl? Doesn't it feel great to buy new clothes? I wore a size 46 jeans, sometimes a 48 and other times a 44. I now wear a 36 and sometimes a 34 depending on the make of the jeans. How are you enjoying those smaller jeans? Isn't it great? Isn't it fun to see old friends and they don't recognize you? I loved that. How about getting those crazy questions like "are you sick?" Yeah, I am sick of being fat. It is a wonderful feeling to know that I did it. I lost 110 pounds. I am a runner now. My life has changed. Can you tell that I am excited? I know you are too because you did it too. Now what?

Maintenance is simply a combination of continuing the physical exercise, whether it be running, walking, biking or whatever you enjoy and food substitution. What do I mean by food substitution?

My biggest food weakness was ice cream. I loved me some ice cream. It was nothing to eat a half gallon while watching the Braves game. There were very few ice cream flavors that I didn't like. In fact, it is easier to list the ones I didn't like instead of the ones I liked. Black Walnut. I didn't like Black Walnut. I can't think of any others. My favorite was probably Chocolate Mint Chip. I learned to like that when I was in my late teens, I worked at the Ice Cream Emporium at Underground Atlanta. That wasn't smart. It was fun, though. My friend, Jeff Thomas, who taught me the Peachtree Road Race ropes, managed the place and several of my friends worked there. That is a whole different story. We won't go there now. You know what was good? Chocolate Mint Chip with Hot Fudge. Lord, have mercy. It wasn't right to work there. I have loved ice cream all my life.

Now that I am maintaining, I have substituted my ice cream cravings with smoothies. I can make a mean, healthy smoothie. My favorite is a banana, natural peanut butter smoothie made with whey powder. It is a great recovery drink after a long run. I have made smoothies with blueberries, strawberries, grape juice, orange juice and chocolate. You can get creative with these. Is it as good as ice cream? It is for me. In fact, it's better.

The only time I have an ice cream is at Chick-fil-A. Their ice cream is low in fat and I don't eat a half gallon. I have learned to substitute foods for maintaining. I can never go back to the way I used to eat. It's not what I do. I mentioned Chick-fil-A. It is my favorite fast food restaurant. Sometimes, I eat a grilled chicken sandwich with a side salad and diet lemonade. Notice 3 substitutes. In the old days, I would have ordered a Chick-fil-A sandwich, waffle fries and a Coke. I now make a substitution and I don't even notice the difference. In fact, I enjoy what I eat now much better.

I eat very little meat. I probably didn't eat 2 pounds of red meat in 18 months. I have had very little pork. I eat turkey, chicken and fish but not very much of any of it. It's almost like I am a cheating vegetarian. I enjoy black beans and brown rice cooked with tomatoes and onions in the crock pot. My favorite is "Daddy Soup." That is vegetable soup featuring big chunks of potatoes. My kids love it, thus the name "Daddy Soup." It is wonderful in cooler weather.

For breakfast, I usually eat a bowl of oatmeal with a banana with milled chia seeds. You should check out chia seeds. I eat lots of bananas and apples. Somewhere, I heard that an apple a day keeps the doctor away. I don't know about that, but fruit is a great substitution for the junk I used to eat. I also enjoy a bowl of grits from time to time. I am, after all, a Southerner.

Why is it that when we drive, we need snacks? It is simply a habit. When we stop to buy gas, we are met with

with all sorts of snack foods. It is funny that we will drive across town to save money on gas and we buy a $1.50 drink and a 99 cent bag of chips. What's up with that? It is a habit. We have to have our snacks while we drive. That being the case, I substitute those chips, honey bun, candy bar or ice cream sandwich with a bag of pretzels. Pretzels have very little fat. If you're alright with the salt intake, they are a great snack. I have cut back on diet sodas to one per day, so depending on whether or not I have had one, I will buy a Coke Zero or Diet Mountain Dew along with my pretzels. I am working on cutting out all diet sodas. Another substitute for chips is sunflower seeds. My goodness, you spend more time cracking the shells than you do eating the seeds. But that is the point, isn't it? It is the habit of munching and this will fulfill the habit for very little food content.

This is not easy if you haven't overcome self but if you have changed your life, it is much easier. People are expecting us to gain the weight back. My goal is to prove them wrong. I am no longer the same. The old self has died and the new self has taken over. Maintenance is a big deal. It is what I will do the rest of my life. It is a great life. Be sure to look me up on Facebook. The group, like the book, is called "All My Strength." There are friends there that will encourage you in your healthy walk. Join us. Let's maintain together.

16 RESOURCES

It is amazing to see how many programs, infomercials and ads there are concerning weight loss. I would imagine that people buy into these or the ads would disappear. I understand why they are popular. We will do most anything to lose weight. The key word being "most." Perhaps, you have heard the story of how a man met a pro golfer and said to him "I would do anything to hit a golf ball like you." The golfer replied "would you get up at 5:00 every morning and hit a thousand golf balls?" What the man was really saying was that he would pay anything to hit a golf ball like a pro golfer but not willing to do the work. That is what people are attempting to do with weight loss gimmicks. They would gladly pay thousands of dollars just to get the weight off. They are looking for the easy way out.

One thing that I am proud of is that I didn't pay anything to lose over 100 pounds. Sure, I bought running clothes and other items to help me along the way, but I never paid any fee for weight loss. I simply decided that I was not going to be fat anymore then began to walk, then run and cut back on food. Too simple, right? It is true. I did it the old fashion way. Exercise and lower food intake.

There are some good references and tools that I used and I want to share those with you. These may not be the best and they may not be for you, but they're the ones I used.

My favorite reference site is Active.com. On this site, you are able to locate activity events in your area. I use it to find running events. Once you choose an event, you can sign up for it right on the site. The results of events are also posted on Active.com. It's pretty cool to see your name listed in an event. I guess it makes me feel like I am reading a box score of a game in which I played. It motivates me. Active.com is loaded with help materials such as what to eat before a race, how to train for a 5k, etc. I don't know how I would have made it through this process without Active.com and it is absolutely free. Do yourself a favor and check out Active.com.

Facebook is not really a weight loss or fitness website, but it was a tool that I used to help motivate me. I kept my friends updated about my process and they responded with positive reinforcement. I can't tell you how exciting it is to hear friends tell you that you are an inspiration to them. Many of my friends followed my lead and began a program of healthy living and weight loss. It makes all the hard work worthwhile just knowing that I made a difference in other's lives. While Facebook is not the only social media site, it is the main one I used and I will never regret it. Facebook provides a place for you to blog and to share with your friends. I posted pictures of myself as the weight was coming off. It is still there and I welcome you to be my Facebook friend and interact with me. It is a good place to ask me questions about my journey. Like I have mentioned previously, we have a group called "All My Strength" that you are welcome to join to discuss healthy living.

WebMD is a nice resource for good health ideas and a reference for things such as injuries. It will happen from time to time. We get injured. I had shin splints in November, 2010. It really slowed me down but WebMD helped me to know how to nurse myself back to running condition. You can also sign up for a WebMD e-mail once a week with all sorts of hints and helps concerning healthy living. I needed all the help I could get.

I have enjoyed the Nike GPS app on my iPhone. It keeps a record of my running. I have my music synched with it as well. It displays a map of the course that is run including color codes for slow and fast pace on the course. You have the option of having your daily runs posted on Facebook and Twitter. I highly recommend this app.

Another great resource of information is *Runner's World* Magazine. You can find it on the internet as well as the traditional magazine. There are many articles in *Runner's World* that will motivate and teach you whether you are an experienced runner or a beginner. I love finding more information concerning healthy and fit living.

There are many resources available to you for free and these are just a few of my favorites. Being involved in physical activity is vital to maintaining a healthy lifestyle both physically and mentally.

17 MY MOTHER LOVED ME

During my weight loss journey, I lost my Mother. I miss her so much. It is important to me that I include a tribute to her. On December 23, 2010, my Mother made her journey to Heaven after dealing with some health issues. It was tough on my sisters, Betty and Patricia, and me. I guess it always is tough to lose a Mom. Even though she was 89 years old, she was sharp mentally and in many ways, it was tougher to deal with because of that sharpness. My Mother always worried about my health. It was rare to visit her without her questioning my weight. "Honey, you need to get that weight off" was the reoccurring theme for most every visit. It really irritated me because nobody wanted to lose weight more than me. She loved me and didn't want me to suffer like my Dad had done. My Dad was a diabetic and always overweight. He passed away at age 53. My Mom didn't want me to go down the same path so she always reminded me. She loved me.

This is the memorial I wrote to honor my Mother for her life celebration:

I grew up in Roswell, Georgia in the days when the population of Roswell was about 2,000 people. Everybody knew everybody. My Dad was a pastor. My 2 sisters are older and left for school before I can remember much so I was like an only child. My Dad not only was a pastor but worked a full time job in Atlanta delivering bread. So, I have many wonderful childhood memories being with my Mother.

My Mother was full of integrity. She would do things just because it was "right." We would live right because that was what you were supposed to do. Right is right and wrong is wrong. She taught me about God's love. She lived a life of God's love. My Mother loved me.

One of my first memories was how she would tell me bedtime stories. My favorite was "The Billy Goats Gruff." No matter what story she told, I would always ask her to tell that one. I also remember having an imaginary friend that I named "Hiffrey." Funny, I have never written that name before. I am not even sure how to spell it, but it was not a made up name. It was Hiffrey's name. How could I make that up? While my Dad thought I may need counseling, my Mother played right along, sometimes making a place for Hiffrey to sit at the table. My Mother loved me.

Mother enjoyed shopping. She loved buying clothes for me. No jeans, however. Her son was going to dress nice at school. I never owned a pair of jeans until I got to college. We would go to Lenox Square, about a 20 mile drive from Roswell, before it was enclosed as a mall. My favorite was our visits to Rich's Department Store. For some reason, I remember looking forward to eating a chili dog and a "cold Coca-Cola" as she always called it at the Rich's cafe. It's funny how some memories stick with you. She loved to shop and I loved being with her. At Christmas time, she would take me to the downtown Rich's to ride the famous Pink Pig. My Mother loved me.

Mother was a great comforter when I was sick. I have so many memories of being sick and her placing a wet washcloth on my forehead, praying for me and sticking right with me through a sick time. She knew how to comfort me. My Mother loved me.

You have heard stories from the "old" days about kids coming home from school after getting a paddling and getting another one by their parents. Not my Mother. If anybody touched me, she would get very upset. She never allowed anyone to lay a hand on her children. That was her responsibility. I never got a paddling at school. I guess I was either a good boy or never got caught, probably never got caught. Good thing we didn't get paddled in college. When I was 16, I got my first traffic ticket. It was for following too close to an emergency vehicle. I wanted to see where the fire was, so I followed the truck. I didn't know what the law was about how close you can get, but I got a ticket. When court time came, there were some high school friends in the courtroom as well with charges a little worse than traffic violations. I was there with my Mother, dressed in a suit for following too close behind a fire truck. My case came first and my Mother stood on my behalf and told the judge what a good boy I was and that I had never given her one minute's worth of trouble. I couldn't help getting a glimpse of my friends sitting there getting ready to find out how their cases would turn out. The judge dropped my charges and we went home. My Mother loved me.

My Dad died at age 53 with diabetes. He always weighed around 300 pounds. He didn't take care of himself. He loved to eat. My Mother never let an opportunity go by to tell me that I needed to lose weight. I have been around 300 most of my adult life. As most of you know, I decided not to be fat anymore and lost over 100 pounds and am living a lifestyle of healthy eating and running. I knew my goal was reached the day I visited her and she said "honey, you don't need to lose any more weight." When I woke up and picked myself off the floor, I called my sisters and told them. Neither one believed my story. My Mother didn't want me to die young like my Dad. I am so glad she lived to see this life change. Though her method was not the best for motivating me, I have no doubt, my Mother loved me.

There is not enough room here to say all I want about my Mother. There are just too many stories. As I reflect on her, I know that the love that she has for me, I also have for my children. It is better understood when you have your own just how much you can love. No matter what my children do, I love them with all of my heart. I learned that from my Mother. My Mother loved me unconditionally.

18 THE GREATEST COMMANDMENT

We live in a time in which we rely upon God's help. One of the more memorable scriptures that I heard growing up was:

Psalm 121:1-2 *I will lift up my eyes to the mountains; From where shall my help come? My help comes from the LORD, Who made heaven and earth.*

How does God help us? I believe that He helps us in many different ways. I am reminded of a sermon series by Andy Stanley, pastor of North Point Community Church in Alpharetta, Georgia. It was a series to encourage us to actually read the Bible. He said that sometimes we ignore phone calls but we always check our text messages. God has sent us a text message and we need to read it. I believe the most important way that God helps us is through His word, the Bible. Where does our help come from? It comes from the Lord who made everything and His word is His text message to us.

His Word is an instruction manual. Have you ever read a manual for a car or a computer and you just didn't get it? I have to be honest. The Bible is the same way. It is amazing how many times I have discovered something "new" in the Bible. Yes, it was there all the time, but for whatever reason, it is either new for me or it takes on a new meaning. As I get older, I am discovering more and more scriptures that I somehow missed the meaning in previous studies. I guess that's why we sometimes call it the "Living Word." It is amazing how a scripture can speak to a situation in my life and many years later, the same scripture will speak a different meaning, both of them in perfect context.

Our American Christian culture has made a big deal out of the Ten Commandments as related to it's being posted in public places. I would love to take a survey among us to see who could actually quote the Ten Commandments. Regardless, we have placed the Ten Commandments as the cornerstone of our belief as a "Christian" nation. However, when Jesus was asked what He thought was the greatest commandment, He didn't choose one of the Ten Commandments.

Mark:12:28 *And one of the scribes came, and heard them questioning together, and knowing that he had answered them well, asked him, What commandment is* *the first of all? 29 Jesus answered, The first is, Hear, O Israel; The Lord our God, the Lord is one: 30 and thou shalt love the Lord thy God with all thy heart, and with all thy soul, and with all thy mind, and with all thy strength. 31 The second is this, Thou shalt love thy neighbor as thyself. There is none other commandment greater than these.*

It is my opinion that God does not help us with these commandments. If He did, what purpose would it serve? He has placed before us commandments for Christ-like living. The key word in all of these is *love*. He does not help us to love. It is a command.

We are to love with all our heart. That is with everything that is dear to us. We are to love with all our soul, which is eternal. We will always have a soul. It never dies. We are to love with our mind. He wants us to study His word and use our minds. When we open our minds, we can hear God speak to us. We are to love with all our strength. What is that all about? This was my "new" revelation and a key to my new life.

How is it that I can love Him with all my strength if I am obese? I had no strength. When I read this with an open mind, I was ashamed of all of the years I had wasted not loving Him with all my strength.

For some reason, in the church, we were never taught this. When I discovered this scripture in light of my personal situation, it changed me. I declared that I would never be fat again and I was going to love Him with all my strength.

Since God does not force me to obey His commandments, I knew that I had to make the choice to change my life. Of course, He helps me understand what it is that I need to do. He enables me. Without Him, I am nothing, but His commandments are there for me to take action. He has laid before me life and death and asks me to choose life. He laid before me blessings and curses and asked me to choose blessings. He gives me choices. It's up to me to choose. I must choose to be a good steward of this temple He has given me.

Jesus tells us to love our neighbor. He says to love one another and to love our enemies. He basically says to love. He does not do it for us. He asks us to do it and leaves it up to us to make it happen. Again, we choose.

God does not force us to praise Him. He would rather force a rock to praise Him than force us do it. God is a God of choice and free will. He puts the destiny and the plan out there for us but we have to do it. He can have the most wonderful plan for our lives but if we don't do it, it won't happen for us. God will raise up another to do it and they will get the reward.

When I began my walking program, I was always mindful of loving Him with my strength. Many times, I would pray as I walked. "God, I praise you with my strength. I love you with my strength. Forgive me for not doing this sooner." Mark 12:30-31 has been my theme scripture throughout my changed life. Who can argue with the greatest commandment? I regret I didn't change my life sooner. There is nothing I can do about that now, so the best is yet to come living an active lifestyle. What about you? You can choose to change your life as well.

19 BREAKING THROUGH THE BARRIER

My blessed Mother pleaded with me most of my life to "get that old weight off." It was understandable. She watched my Dad die with diabetes at age 53, just before my Mother's 50th birthday. As I mentioned in the tribute to my Mother, she loved me. She didn't want to see me die at an early age. However, her method was not successful. I already knew that I needed to lose weight. She did not need to tell me. There were very few visits with her that she didn't mention my weight. I didn't like hearing it. I knew that I needed to lose weight and that method wasn't working with me.

In this book, I decided that I would tell my story and hope that it makes a difference in your life. So, if you are already motivated or don't want to hear a sermon, you have my permission to skip this chapter.

Do you remember being a child, not knowing how people could ride a bike? You had training wheels on your bike and had no problem riding but the very thought of riding a bike without training wheels was incomprehensible. But, there was this one day that you attempted to ride the bike without training wheels and you did it. How exciting was that? From that day forward, it was never a mystery as to how to ride a bike. I went 30 years without riding a bike and just recently bought a bike. I didn't need training wheels for a while, I just rode the bike like I always had. I had broken through the barrier of comprehension when I was a child and I am still there.

1 Corinthians 13:12: *"For now we see through a glass, darkly; but then face to face: now I know in part; but then shall I know even as also I am known."*

In this life, we cannot comprehend all of the ways of God. It is a mystery. It was just like looking at people ride a bike when we could not comprehend how it works. However, once we broke through the barrier of comprehension, it was easy. When we die, we will break through that barrier and realize all that we need to comprehend about this current life.

The best way for me to explain my life change is tell you there is a comprehension barrier that I broke through. For most of my life, I was on the outside looking in with no belief that I could change. Sure, I lost weight many times but it was always a struggle. Once I broke through, it was no longer a struggle because I was on the inside looking out. It is like being able to ride a bike with no training wheels. It was easy. It is like being in Heaven looking back on this life. Full comprehension. I broke through the barrier.

I hope this is an encouragement for you. It seems tough. It seems impossible. It is incomprehensible that you could ever change your life and become fit. But, if you are really disgusted with your life and you decide to change, you can break through the barrier. That is why it is easy for me now.

I have challenges every day but I never consider giving up and going back. Most people who lose weight gain it back. That is because they only went on a diet like I did for so many years. Once I broke through the barrier, I became a new person.

What about you? Nobody can push you through the barrier. If I could, I would. My Mother tried pushing me through but it just doesn't work that way. I had to decide to do it. Once you are disgusted enough to make a decision for fitness and healthy living and you are serious about it, you can be on the inside looking out instead of the outside looking in. You can change! You can do it! You won't regret it, I promise. Join me on the other side of the barrier. It is so rewarding and enjoyable.

Christian friends, here is my sermon: I am not judging your Christianity because it is not a requirement for salvation. Our bodies are the temple of the Holy Spirit. It is a serious matter to take care of this temple the Lord has given us. If He loaned us a house for a month, would we trash the place or leave it cleaner than when we arrived? He has loaned us this body for a unknown time. We should be good stewards of this body He has loaned us. I have not been a good steward. I abused my body for many years and for that, I asked forgiveness.

My goal is to keep this body fit and healthy to the best of my ability and with all my strength.

I would love to see you to live a healthy life. I really would. I want you to experience what I have experienced. I have enjoyed seeing family and friends that haven't seen me since my weight loss and them not recognizing me. I have enjoyed shopping for Large shirts instead of XXXL shirts. It is amazing to get up early on a Saturday morning and run 6 miles without stopping. I want you to enjoy some of these things as well. It is a great life.

My hope for you is that you will have a crisis moment, if that is what it takes. I hope you get disgusted and make a decision to change. I hope that you can live the day that changes your life like I did. When Dr. Brown told me that the first symptom of a heart attack is a heart attack, it changed my life. It may not change yours, but if you don't do something to change the direction of your life, you may not get to enjoy your grandchildren. How many obese 70 year old people do you know?

I realize I can't create your crisis moment. I wish that I could. When I see obese people of my faith at conferences and meetings, my heart breaks. I know that they are not living God's intended life for them. I know they are not happy with their life. He designed them to be healthy and active. They are miserable inside like I was.

I finally realized it on July 16, 2009 and have lived it ever since. I wasted many years that I am so sorry for, but I changed my life. What about you? If I did it, you can do it. That's a promise. You may not use my method but you can change your life.

Jim Rohn says **"You cannot change your destination overnight, but you can change your direction overnight."**

Now, it is up to you. I hope that you will make the change and love God with *all your strength*. You will not be disappointed, I promise.

ACKNOWLEDGEMENTS

There are too many people to thank and it is difficult to acknowledge all of them here. I will certainly leave out some people. Obviously, my immediate family, Cathy, Marie, Missi and Tiffany who tolerated hearing me talk about losing weight and running to the point they were sick of me. I appreciate them understanding that I had to be obsessed with this for it to work. I have a great big extended family that I appreciate as well. Many of them have encouraged me along the way, including Paul Conn, who graciously wrote the foreword. I have run several races with my wonderful family. My friends have been incredible supporters, especially my best friend, Jeff Pace. He has been my best accountability supporter and my faithful friend. Lee University and Roswell High School friends and "All My Strength" Facebook group friends have been so supportive of my efforts. I am a blessed man with so many family members and friends. I love and appreciate all of you. I acknowledge Jesus Christ, who is my strength. Thank you, Lord, for bringing me to the place where I had to make a decision.